Different Dreams

Reflections and Realities of Raising a
Child with Developmental Disabilities

MARY KAY DEGENOVA, PH.D.

ISBN: 978-1-4834-7069-6 (sc)
ISBN: 978-1-4834-7070-2 (e)

Library of Congress Control Number: 2017909058

Lulu Publishing Services rev. date: 07/07/2017

For Louis and Ella, my two biggest teachers

Humanity will be able to live only if we

discover that our differences are a treasure.

—Jean Vanier

INTRODUCTION

The idea for this book began in a pediatric neurology waiting room. I was there for a routine checkup for my eighteen-year-old son, Louis, who has developmental disabilities. While I had been in that waiting room countless times over the course of Louis's life, this day was different. Sitting across from me was a mother cradling a newborn in her arms. She wiped away slight tears on her face as she looked around the room at the other kids, some of whom were running around while others were in wheelchairs with feeding tubes. The look on her face brought back all of my emotions from my first neurology visit with Louis. She reminded me so much of myself when I first began this journey.

In my own case, my pregnancy was typical. It lasted nine months, and my husband and I were excited and felt ready to become parents. Everything was going as planned. That is until five minutes before Louis was born when he suffered a stroke while in the birth canal. He wasn't breathing when he was born, yet he was quickly resuscitated and thought to be just fine. I remember being so relieved and grateful to hear his first cry. I called my parents to tell them I had just delivered a perfectly healthy baby boy.

The subsequent call to them an hour later was really hard. Louis started having nonstop seizures shortly after birth and spent the next two weeks in neonatal intensive care. The doctors eventually told us the stroke caused a significant amount of brain damage.

Louis was just three weeks old when he had his first neurology visit, which, to this day, is seared in my mind. I will never forget my feelings, the room, the other mothers and children, and even what I was wearing. In that moment, I knew my life was going in a direction I could not have imagined. I had little control over it. I remember wanting to bolt out of the waiting room, telling myself this couldn't be happening to me. I had a plan laid out for my life, and having a child with brain damage wasn't part of it. I was terrified I didn't have what it took to raise a child with disabilities. I didn't even know what that meant. I was hoping my child wouldn't need as much care as some of the other children in the waiting room, and I hated myself for thinking those thoughts. There was so much I didn't know, and I didn't even know which questions I needed to ask. I was scared, confused, exhausted, and angry.

And if one more person told me, "God chooses only special moms for special children," I was going to scream! Yet I was supposed to be really happy because I was a new mom. I had a baby. I had to force myself to smile.

I also remember the other moms smiling at my son and me. They were older moms who had been living the life of neurology waiting rooms for years. They all seemed so at ease and capable of caring for their children. They seemed so strong. That day, they were sending me, through their smiles, the same message I was transferring to the woman sitting across from me in the waiting room who inspired this book: It's going to be okay.

During that first appointment, the neurologist tried to prepare me for a child who may never walk, talk, or feed himself. I left that visit in shock with a newborn in my arms, wondering how I was going to best care for my son and where life was taking us.

I could have never anticipated on that day all the incredible moments and places this journey has afforded my family and me. I did become one of those smiling, strong moms in the waiting room. I have strength as a mother I never thought possible. While I would have never chosen this path, if I had a choice, I wouldn't change it now. It has enriched my life immensely and has brought many gifts; however, it hasn't always been easy.

Louis is a thriving, happy, eighteen-year-old young man now, but not without his challenges. His primary diagnoses are cerebral palsy, autism, epilepsy, and intellectual disability. He will be in high school until he is twenty-one, and then we hope to find productive and meaningful work for him. He will always require care, but he has surpassed so many of our expectations from that first neurology visit. He walks, runs, and even rides a bike. He does speak, although it is often difficult to understand him. He has learned to use all kinds of electronic devices to make himself known. He is also somewhat typical, as he loves playing golf with my husband, watching sports on television, and bugging his younger sister, Ella. Mostly he loves people with all his heart, and once you are with him, you feel it.

Now I feel like a veteran who has learned so much from trial and error and years of talking with and listening to other parents. This book is an attempt to let other parents know what the journey may be like and what one could expect, both good and bad. I've included what worked for me and other mothers as well as what our biggest mistakes were.

While all our families and children are unique, and no two families and children with developmental disabilities act the same way, I do believe we share commonalities and experiences in raising our children. This book may not make it to the woman who sat across from me in the waiting room, but I hope that it reaches someone who finds it of use.

While this probably isn't a path most parents want to find themselves on, it is a path filled with fabulous people—individuals who have learned what is most important in life; persons who have given up the pursuit of perfection and chosen the joy of acceptance; people who know there are many ways to be a valuable member of society; and men and women who understand the precious insights and gifts that come from raising a child with a developmental disability.

Make Time to Grieve

Grief is a difficult topic. It begins this book because I believe it is a part of the opening chapter of your new life that should not be ignored, glossed over, or stuffed to the back. It needs to be addressed up front and acknowledged. It is natural and normal to grieve the loss of what you expected parenthood to be, while at the same time being grateful and loving your child unconditionally.

The process of grief starts at different times for families. For some parents, the knowledge that a child has a genetic or neurological development issue, such as

Down syndrome (trisomy 21), comes with results from a test before birth. For others like me, the realization comes at birth. Still others spend months and years possibly wondering if their child might have delayed or atypical development based on behavior. Whether it's before, at, or years following birth, once parents get a diagnosis of their child having a developmental disability, it is oftentimes gut-wrenching, causing great mental and emotional pain.

As difficult as it was to hear a painful diagnosis about my child, it was surprisingly easy to push the grief associated with it aside and pretend it didn't exist. I had tremendous grief that I stuffed deep down inside in order to put on a good face of how strong and capable I was at handling the news. I was also driven to figure out what I needed to do to best meet the needs of my son. The intensity of that focus actually allowed me to keep my grief at bay. I told myself I didn't have time to stop and grieve. I was too busy figuring out my next move.

My grief eventually caught up with me, and I knew I needed to process my anger, disappointment, and fear. I eventually reached out to a mom who had a child with trisomy 9, and we became close friends and confidants. We were a safe place for each other to vent all of our emotions.

Don't let your feelings fester inside. Whether a formal support group, a friend, a therapist, or your journal, find a place you feel comfortable releasing your emotions without judgment. You're probably not feeling anything another parent has not experienced before.

Out of all the topics I discussed with other parents regarding children with disabilities, grief was the touchiest. Parents did not like talking or, at times, even thinking about their own grief. I've learned this grief is a complicated one that changes and evolves over a life span. It takes courage and commitment to face it, and while some parents feel they resolved their grief quickly, others admit they have never really stopped mourning.

The grief associated with having a child with a developmental disability is often different from a more typical grief such as the loss of a loved one. Both are challenging and can be overwhelming, but when you grieve a loved one who has passed away, there is an expected pattern. Not everyone will follow that model, but one exists. People tend to bring food, send sympathy cards, and attend ceremonial rituals such as funerals or wakes where people express their condolences and offer you their love and support. There is an expected period of mourning during which people will anticipate a range of emotional behavior, and after that, people hope you start moving on. Throughout this period of mourning, you are expected to be depressed and express sorrow, and friends will often ask you about your grief.

In contrast, when you have a child with developmental disabilities, many people feel uncomfortable asking questions. They don't know what to say or are afraid they'll speak the wrong thing, so they often avoid talking. Many parents I talked with expressed how lonely they felt in their grief because family and friends didn't want to talk about the disability.

In addition, this grief may be a lifelong process as parents need to frequently readjust their expectations as their child grows and changes. For example, when my son was eight, he developed an uncontrollable seizure disorder seemingly out of the blue. Louis hadn't had a seizure since the first few days of his life, so I wasn't planning on him being epileptic, even though I knew that many children with brain damage have seizures.

When the neurologist told me my son had epilepsy, I felt like I was punched in the stomach, and it set me back to almost the same feelings I had when Louis was born. I didn't know how this was going to change our lives and what it meant for my son and my family, but I recognized it was going to be more difficult. Until that point, I had gotten good at knowing what to expect from my son's behavior and creating a school and family pattern that worked well for all of us. Having seizures was a new, scary territory for me that ultimately did change our lives significantly.

Louis continues to have uncontrollable seizures to this day, even after he has tried over ten years of different medicines. We still continue to try new things but with guarded optimism. I don't want to get my hopes up too high when we try a new medicine or procedure to control his seizures because I have been let down so many times. I have learned that, with every new setback or unmet expectation, I needed to readjust and grieve, sometimes just a little and other times a lot.

The mom of a sixteen-year-old son with Down syndrome once told me how hard it was for her when all the kids in his high school class were learning to drive. The other moms in the class were talking about how much they both loved and hated having their sons drive. She went home from school that day, locked herself in a closet so no one could see her, and sobbed. She was shocked at her own behavior, as she had felt everything was going very well for them. For reasons she cannot explain, on that day with that conversation about driving, she could not hold back the floodgate of tears.

I understand what this mother was going through. Twinges of grief still come for me when I think about my son not going to college, getting married, or having children (and making me a grandmother to his kids). No one has ever asked me how I am doing with that grief. No one even knows it's there. I've grieved my daughter not having a brother who can talk to her and help her in typical ways when she needs it. Sometimes I just wonder what kind of person he would be and what he would be doing if he didn't have brain damage.

Then I think how much I would miss the person he has become and the individual who I have become because of the disability. This is the paradox. We can love our children immensely for the people they are and be overwhelmingly grateful for whom they have helped us become, yet we can still grieve for the people they could have been. Gratefulness and grief are not mutually exclusive.

Amid the grief that might be short or long term, that could be overwhelming at times or completely resolved, remember that both you and your child are good enough. Whatever may lie ahead, your thinking and feelings will shape your experience. I always remind myself that what I sought most in life—love, belonging, purpose, and community—I have found in my child with developmental disabilities. It's wrapped in lots of uniqueness, frustration, and uncertainty, but it is there, and it is beautiful!

Helpful Suggestions

- Acknowledge the grief.
- Recognize that grieving can be a lonely process. Find someone to talk with about your feelings.
- Spend time and talk with other parents who have children with disabilities.
- Understand that grief may be a lifelong process that is altered as situations and expectations change.

- Allow yourself to feel all of your feelings without judgment.

- Try not to turn your grief inward on yourself or direct it at others. Instead write down your feelings in a journal to get them out.

- Realize that grieving takes time. Set aside time to process your feelings.

REST WHEN YOU CAN

A child with developmental disabilities requires extra time and attention that other people don't necessarily see. Not only do you have all the typical parenting responsibilities, you may have, in addition, seemingly endless doctor and therapy appointments. Add to that the time worrying over the future, grieving, and trying to figure out how you are going to manage physically, mentally, and financially—not to mention whatever health issues are going on. The list is endless, and you may feel emotionally and physically exhausted already. Remember two things: You only have so much time, energy, and emotional resilience; and it's a marathon, not a sprint. Pace yourself.

I honestly didn't know what fatigue was until my son was born. I know now because I am no longer depleted. For the first years of Louis's life, I was exhausted. First of all, it felt like he never slept more than twenty minutes at a time. I am sure he did, but my husband and I felt we were up and down all through the night. We became so tired that even trying to figure a way out was too exhausting, so we just kept going.

One night, Louis slept through the night entirely. My husband and I woke up the next morning, looked at the clock, and gasped in fear. We both thought he had died during the night. We frantically ran into his room, only to find him sleeping peacefully. Something abruptly changed in his patterns, and to this day, I still don't know what it was, but I do know it was a needed change for us. Once we started sleeping through the night, life became more manageable.

I'm sure other people saw my fatigue, and when they asked if I needed help, I probably said no and told them I was fine. I have always been bad about asking for and accepting help. For me, I think trying not to need others came not from strength but from fear of being vulnerable. When people offered help, I should have accepted. When they didn't, I should have asked. We all need help raising our children, and having a child with a disability requires even more support. You can only do so much, and if you're exhausted and in a constant state of worry and anxiety, you can do much less.

There was support I could have used sooner than I did, had I accessed those resources. For example, many states and local agencies have some sort of respite program that grants funding to families to hire a caretaker for a certain period of time. Its intended use is for parents to get a break from the demands of caring for their child with disabilities. I did eventually start using child-care services and agency drop-off programs. These were vital in helping me get more rest and take those needed breaks we all need from parenting.

You may experience a fatigue that is so engulfing it prevents you from making good decisions and being kind to yourself and others. You may say you don't have time to rest or can't afford a childcare or respite provider. Or if you do get help, you need to do more important things than rest and replenish yourself. This is not a good long-term plan because you will eventually burn out or get sick.

Find out early on what resources are available in your area by checking with local agencies serving children with disabilities. Ask for help when you need it and get the rest you need. Nothing is more important than your health and peace of mind. If you lose that, both your child and you have lost something critical.

Helpful Suggestions

- Rest when you can.
- Find out about respite services in your state.
- Relinquish some control to others who can help.
- Plan ahead for "me time" by making a date with yourself, and schedule it on your calendar, just like any other important meeting.
- Make your own well-being a priority.
- Forgive yourself for not being able to do everything. You don't need to.

FIND A COMMUNITY

While you may have a lot of other support, nothing matches the encouragement of other parents who understand more fully what you are going through. Finding a group of moms who had children with developmental disabilities was vital for my well-being. Not only were they an important source of information, they helped me cope and made me laugh as there is a lot of humor along this path. Other parents are out there, and they will welcome you with open and nonjudgmental arms. Find them, and be honest with them. You are not feeling anything they have not experienced before. And remember—while you have a lot to learn from them, you also have much to teach.

In Louis's first two years of life, before I reached out to other moms who had children with disabilities, on many days I felt completely isolated and alone. I had many friends, but my long-term friends couldn't relate to what I was going through. Some were so afraid they would say the wrong thing that they would hardly speak anything at all about parenthood. Some felt they couldn't share anything about their typically developing children because they feared it might upset me. Thus, playdates and social gatherings became awkward.

Without my good female friends to vent to, I began using my husband for my dumping ground of all my feelings of fear and inadequacy in raising our son. This soon became problematic for many reasons:

1. He was dealing with his own feelings in his own way of what parenthood would mean for him. He didn't need me piling on my feelings for hours after he returned home from work.

2. It wasn't good for either of us to spend what little time we had together focused exclusively on my feelings about raising our son.

3. Regardless of the circumstance, my husband could have never been the girlfriend I needed him to be. I needed to find some new friends.

Don't be like me and wait two years before finding a community of other mothers raising children with developmental disabilities. Most hospitals have support groups available for moms, dads, and siblings of special needs children. Many therapists know of both formal and informal groups for families. I needed to be asking about group support early on to all the many health professionals coming through my life.

I found a group once my son started a special education preschool. At drop-off one day, one of the other moms at the school suggested a standing meeting time at a nearby coffee shop for any moms who could make it. It became a very important group for all who regularly attended. Had another mom not suggested it, I hope I would have asked the school to organize something.

If you find yourself in a community that doesn't have a group, start one. Other parents will thank you for taking this initiative. One way to start a group is to talk to special education teachers, doctors, and therapists in your community and ask them to spread the word about a new group forming. Another way is to use the Internet to create a meet-up group using a community-based website specifically designed to get people connected. Also contact local agencies designated to help families with special needs children and ask them to help form a group that works for you.

There are also many Internet groups, blogs, and e-mail lists that are valuable to be a part of. Some of these are listed in the resource section at the back of the book. However, while a virtual community may be more convenient and a great source of information, the human connection to other parents and the intimacy that comes from sharing emotions can't be replicated on the computer.

I am part of many different groups now, and each time we meet, I go away surprised and enriched from the conversations. I always learn something new. Without these other parents, I couldn't have raised my son with as much strength and laughter. They have been some of the most amazing and resourceful people I have ever met and have been some of the biggest blessings along the way.

However, in addition to finding a community of parents of children with disabilities, don't neglect your long-term friendships. Fight against the urge to withdraw from contact with old friends in order to make room for new friends. You need both. You are a person with more interests and dimension than being a parent raising a child with special needs. Don't let it define you, as it can't be all about your child all the time. Don't lose yourself and that which you loved about yourself in your parenting journey.

Helpful Suggestions

- Ask health professionals about existing support groups.

- Start a support group if you can't find one to meet your needs.

- Join a group of other parents raising children with special needs.

- Allow yourself to both learn and teach in support groups.

- Maintain your long-term friendships that don't center around children with disabilities.

- Remember to laugh.

Find the Right Health Care Professionals and Programs

You will probably have the opportunity to get to know more doctors and therapists than you ever wanted. Some you will like; others you will not. It is important to find doctors and therapists who are a good fit for both you and your child, particularly if you anticipate having a long-term relationship. If insurance and resources allow for options, ask other parents who they do and don't like, and don't be afraid to switch if it isn't a good fit.

You will probably see therapists, such as those working with speech and fine and gross motor skills, more than you will see doctors. While you might be able to put up with a doctor whom you are not fond of, it will be more difficult with therapists. If you are like me, you will meet some that become like well-loved family members and others that leave you frazzled.

Remember that therapists do not know your child like you do; nor do they know your own unique story. They are only looking at a particular area in your child, while you are dealing with the whole child and family system. It's a therapist's job to try to get you to do a certain amount of therapy between visits. It's your responsibility to be realistic in what can get accomplished in a few days or weeks.

I've learned to always ask the therapists, "If I only have five minutes a day to focus on this therapy, what should I do?" or "What are the three most important things to focus on?" It may be that your child is involved in five other types of therapies, and if you gave thirty minutes a day to each therapy, you wouldn't get anything else done. Yes, therapy is important, but so is your sanity and the health of the family at large. Share with the therapists the other demands on both your and your child's time, and be realistic about what can get accomplished in a day. If resources permit, ask if there are students who need experience working with children with disabilities who could implement some of the exercises. Usually therapists know of someone who would love to help and needs the work.

State funds are often available to help enhance the development of a child with special needs through early intervention, therapy, and after-school programs. As soon as you have confirmation that your child has a disability, find out what resources and funding exist in your community and state. The easiest way to do this is to call your state's Department of Mental Health and ask for the number to the Developmental Disability office. It's easy to find these numbers on the Internet, and every state should have one. Once you have made contact with the developmental disability liaison, the ball gets rolling. Typically a social worker will do an intake and assessment and find out what services you need and give you information about which services are available.

Authorized by law, all states have an early intervention program for children with disabilities. The Individuals with Disabilities Education Act (IDEA) requires it, and it can be found in Part C of IDEA. These programs can be called many things, such as Part C or First Steps, but they all operate basically the same way. They provide services from birth to usually age three for children with disabilities or developmental delays. Programs typically focus on skills that relate to physical, cognitive, communication, social/emotional, and self-help.

If an infant or toddler has a disability or a developmental delay in one or more of these developmental areas, that child will likely be eligible for early intervention services. Services may include assistive technology; audiology and hearing; speech, occupational, and physical therapy; nutrition and medical services; and psychological services. However, all states define developmental delay differently. It's important to understand your state's definition.

You can find your state's early intervention program by asking your pediatrician and local hospital about early intervention services or going to the federal government website (www.cdc.gov) and searching developmental disabilities. This website provides many links to other state and federal programs you may find useful.

You can also obtain a lot of information by going to Parent Center Hub (www.parentcenterhub.org). This website summarizes the early intervention system in your state and presents the basics to get you started. It is worth your while to call many different organizations along with federal agencies to see what is available for you.

Finally, when you are working with professionals, don't be hesitant to ask about the cost of things. If you are like most parents who have a child with disabilities, you're worried about finances. You are not a bad parent if you ask how much a drug, therapy tool, or test costs and if there is a cheaper alternative or discount. I always ask about the price and refuse to feel shame for it. I have overspent many times with huge co-pays, tests not covered by insurance, or therapy tools I could have done without. In almost all of those situations, there was a cheaper alternative or a discount, but I just didn't know which questions to ask to get there. Ask several questions. It's your right.

I always ask health care professionals these questions when something new is suggested: Is it necessary? Will it change any outcome? How much is the expected cost? The last question prompts two more related questions: Is there a cheaper alternative? Do you know of any discount or coupon available?

I then check with my insurance company and make the decision based on the information available at the time. In addition, whenever I pay a bill such as to a hospital or doctor's office, I ask if there is a discount for paying in full or about a payment plan. These questions have saved me thousands of dollars over the years without sacrificing care for my child.

Helpful Suggestions

- Seek other parents' opinions about doctors and therapists.

- Ask someone to join you at important appointments to help take notes, record discussions, and interpret the information.

- Ask therapists what is most important to focus on.

- Be realistic about how much you can get accomplished in a day.

- Ask questions about the cost of things and if there is a cheaper alternative, coupon, or discount.

- Research federal, state, and local resources.

Raise the Bar

Some of the best advice I got early on was from a special education teacher. She told me to try to raise my child as if he were typically developing and have expectations that are similar to those of his peers. She gave me countless examples of well-meaning parents tolerating and even encouraging age-inappropriate behavior. She would often remind me that children with developmental disabilities are not "cute" or "adorable" past the age of a typically developing child being so.

For example, if it is inappropriate for a typically developing adolescent to try to kiss a stranger or teacher, it should be unsuitable for an adolescent with developmental disabilities. While this behavior may be difficult to control, it should not be blatantly tolerated just because the child has a disability.

This special education teacher has spent years trying to help parents understand that the child's disability should not get in the way of effective parenting as all children need discipline, boundaries, and clear expectations. She has taught me that disabilities are often separate from behavior, and it's important to keep them distinct in your mind. For example, if a parent wouldn't allow a typically developing child to get his or her way by crying or throwing a fit, then neither should he or she permit a child with developmental disabilities. Behaviors are often learned and reinforced— not necessarily the result of a child having a disability.

Our children can and often do surprise us. Start off by always assuming your child can do more than you actually think he or she can. Then, if necessary, you can always modify your expectations to be more realistic. If you expect your child to learn to wait patiently or to wash his own face, then he or she will be more likely to develop that skill. If you never expect it, your child may not reach that ability level. While all our children have different ability levels and we need to celebrate those skills, they all need expectations. Our children are also creatures of habit, and while discipline and routines may be frustrating to implement and skills painstakingly difficult to develop, once in place, they can make life much easier for both you and your child.

In my case, we have an expectation in the house that everyone cleans up after himself or herself after dinner. This entails dealing with napkins, rinsing the dish and getting it in the dishwasher, wiping the area where he or she ate, and washing hands before leaving the kitchen. It sounds simple enough, but Louis struggles with most of it. He sometimes drops a dish on the way to the sink or leaves large chunks of food on the plate after rinsing.

It would be much easier and less of a mess if I just did it for him, which I used to do more often than I like to admit. My daughter holds me accountable, as she often reminds me that, if she has to do it every day, so should her brother, even if it is in a modified attempt. And she has been right about this. While progress is slow and messes are common, Louis has consistently gotten better at it. More importantly though, he now knows it's a nonnegotiable expectation.

Another example is requiring Louis to help make his own school lunch. This would be much faster and easier if I would do it all myself, yet I require his sister to make her own. He still cannot do all his lunch, like peel an orange or close a Ziploc bag, but he has learned to spread peanut butter and jelly and assemble ham and cheese on bread. It might not be pretty, and it might make a big mess that he has to help clean up, but it gives him a sense of pride and teaches him important life skills.

I have found it helpful when trying to raise the bar to get other people involved. As with most children, yours will perform differently for a parent than he or she would for someone else. For example, childcare providers have managed to get my child to bed by himself without any fuss while it was an epic battle for me. Therapists have taught my son skills that I actually could have taught him myself if he hadn't adamantly refused to cooperate with me.

I have countless examples of me thinking his disability was the cause of him not being able to do something, but in reality, he just wouldn't do it for my husband or me because he was so skillful at manipulating us. We needed to have the bar raised higher in many circumstances and not fall back so quickly on his disability being the reason he couldn't do something.

Just like most people, children with developmental disabilities never stop learning. Figure out the strategies and tools your child needs to learn best, and then be prepared to constantly change as your child transforms. Don't ever give up believing in their ability to learn, grow, and reach new heights. It is amazing what our children can rise to.

Helpful Suggestions

- Don't let your child's disability get in the way of effective parenting.
- Have your behavioral expectations in line with appropriate age levels and keep them high.

- Assume your child can do more than you actually think he or she can.

- Get other people involved in helping to raise the bar.

- Figure out strategies and tools to keep your child learning new skills.

- Remember that behaviors are often learned and reinforced.

FIND A BALANCE YOU
CAN LIVE WITH

Not long after I received the news that my newborn had

brain damage, I went into fix-it mode. I had heard over

and over that the first five years of brain development

were the most important for making important pathways,

and I vowed to do everything I could to help my child

succeed. I scoured every book I could get my hands on

and investigated every program and type of therapy.

Looking back on it now, I can see I was frantic and

in a crazy-busy syndrome in order to avoid looking at

my own life. I was trying to make the diagnosis go

away, prove everyone wrong, and find a way to make things better and more in line with my expectations for parenthood. This is one of my biggest regrets: I didn't spend more time just relaxing and loving my child.

These two things don't necessarily have to be at odds. It's possible that a parent can read everything to educate himself or herself and at the same time enjoy the life of the child. I encourage families to research and explore all different types of ways for their child to have a more typical life and to become knowledgeable about their child's disability, but don't be frantic in that pursuit. Find a healthy balance between doing nothing and being crazy busy. Help your child reach his or her full potential while enjoying who your child is and the gifts that come with the challenges.

Know that it is almost impossible to strike the perfect balance between doing too much and not enough, between working for change and accepting what is. The shoulds, coulds, and woulds can be forever haunting. I did the best I could at the time, and I try not to dwell on not taking more time to enjoy the beauty and joy of my child in my arms.

The developmental disability will probably always be there, manifesting itself in all different forms of which you will have little control, but the innocence and beauty of a child is so fleeting. My advice is to enjoy and savor it. Don't let anxiety about the future taint the joys you can experience today. Try to strike a good balance, and at the end of the day, know that you did the best you could.

I did manage to become knowledgeable and participate in many programs and therapies designed to help children with developmental disabilities. I am sure some helped our son, but others I will never be sure about. For example, when Louis was three years old, we decided to go to Cleveland, Ohio, for three weeks for him to participate in an electric stimulation procedure to increase awareness and use of his tongue. It was experimental, not covered by insurance, and met with resistance from his neurologist at the time. The procedure proved to be extremely helpful for Louis, and after two weeks, he stuck his tongue out of his mouth for the first time. Today, that procedure is used in many hospitals, and some insurance policies cover it.

However, other times we decided not to pursue new therapies that we learned about or were suggested by a health care professional. What I try to do in making these decisions is to educate myself, weigh all the pros and cons for the entire family, listen to my gut, and make the best decision I can at the time.

New programs and therapies for children with developmental disabilities seem to pop up all the time. Some are conventional and covered by most insurance; others are extremely controversial. There will be numerous new programs, treatments, and devices that will promise to cure your child. There will be testimonies from other parents about the amazing results achieved with their child. However, no two children are alike, and there is probably no quick fix for any of our children.

No doctor, therapist, or other parent knows your child better than you do. Go with what makes sense for you and your family. Some programs and therapies may be too expensive and time-consuming to be manageable. Others may be exactly what your child needs, and you are willing to make whatever sacrifice you can to get your child that help. Someone may criticize you about whatever choices you make, but no one except you and your family knows your story and all you are managing. Find the system that works best for all of you and work at keeping it.

Helpful Suggestions

- Check in with yourself often about keeping a healthy balance for you and your family.
- Work on helping your child reach his or her potential while simply enjoying your child.
- Choose programs and therapies that make sense for you and your family.
- Remember that no one knows your child better than you do.

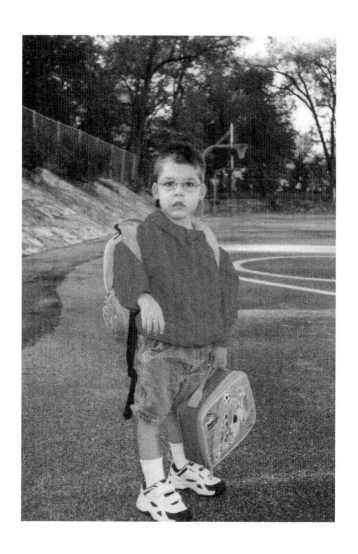

Give Up Some Control

Life is scary for all of us at times. It's frightening raising any child and letting him or her go, but it is a normal part of both parenting and growing up. We need to let our children learn from their mistakes and take appropriate risks. Try not to deny your child with a disability this typical life passage, as painful as it may be for you. While the circumstances may be different and the downfall could be more costly, our children need to make their own mistakes and learn from them. When you can, let them leap into new experiences, even if you are terrified for them.

For me as a parent, letting go of Louis was a thousand times harder than letting go of his sister. What if the world were mean to him? What if there were no one around to help him? What if he fell and got hurt? What if no one understood him? What if he were afraid? I could "what if" all day long, but in the end, it is his world to inherit, and he has to learn to navigate it.

Only you know what risks are worth taking for you and your child and what potential cost/benefit ratio is right for you. When opportunities come along—and they will—try to live a little outside of your comfort zone and see what is possible for your child. Others will have ideas that may sound out of the question for you initially, but allow those suggestions to at least percolate. Try to get at the core of your resistance. If you are seriously worried about safety, then you should just say no. If you are worried that your child won't be cared for in the same way as you do for him or her, maybe you should reconsider. While you may be the best caretaker of your child, other people can tend to your child, even though it may not be in the exact way you would like.

A good example of this is summer camp. There are countless summer camp opportunities for children with developmental disabilities. Many are offered at a very affordable cost to families, and programs exist to help defray those costs. Check with local agencies to see if funding exists for summer camps because some states offer summer camp vouchers.

If a week of summer camp is something you would consider for a typically developing child, you should contemplate it for your child with developmental disabilities. Many children are scared to go to a sleepover camp for the first time, and your child with a disability may be frightened too. You may be anxious, but try not to let your fear keep you from allowing your child that experience.

The first time Louis went away to sleepover camp, he was ten years old. It was a well-staffed camp for children with developmental disabilities, and they assured me they were trained to handle almost any situation. I was anxious even thinking about letting him go off to some strange place with people he didn't know for five nights. Other moms convinced me that I needed to let him go and said he would love it. Taking their advice, I packed him up.

He screamed, cried, and kicked the whole drive to camp. He pulled out all the stops. As we neared the camp, he pretended he was sick. I actually thought he may indeed be sick and I should turn around. I didn't though, and once we arrived, I had to physically drag him out of the car. I felt like a horrible mother.

Along with feeling horrible, after I dropped him off, I felt like part of my body had been cut off. I felt lost without him. It was a rude and painful awakening that I had spent so much time focused on his needs that I had lost an important part of myself. I knew it wasn't a healthy relationship for either of us and I had to give up more control. I couldn't keep him sheltered from the outside world. He was going to be afraid, he has going to know discomfort, and he was going to experience cruelty just like any other kid. He was also going to experience being able to be separate from Mom, knowing he could get through the night without my help and there are other people in the world who can help. Camp proved to be a valuable and insightful experience for both of us.

Louis has come to love his camp experiences, even though the first one was a little rocky. We have learned he can go away from home for a week and be just fine.

He has gotten to experience such joys as sitting around campfires, eating s'mores, zip-lining, canoeing, fishing, mud-slinging, sleeping in a cabin, and making new friends. He is always so excited to share with his family all the fun he had. He comes home dirty, tired, and happy to see us again, just like any other kid. Best of all, he has learned to be more independent, and we are all thrilled about that.

Helpful Suggestions

- When you can, allow your child to take age-appropriate risks.
- Be curious about your resistance in allowing your child to try new things.
- Allow other people to care for your child, even though it would not be in the exact way you prefer.

- Investigate programs for your child that would encourage more independence.

- Try to give up some control where you can.

Pay Attention to the Rest of Your Family

Raising a child with developmental disabilities can create a unique and complicated family environment. This is particularly true if you have other children. Louis's sister, Ella, who is two years younger than he is, has been my biggest teacher in this issue.

One regret I have in parenting is that I should have tried harder to give just as much attention to Ella as I did to Louis. I knew this going into parenting my second child as I had read books about siblings of special needs children, but I still couldn't, wouldn't, or just didn't implement it. I told myself there wasn't enough time and that Louis needed more attention than Ella did. For example, I assumed someone had to try to teach Louis how to walk, while Ella could figure it out on her own. I could replace the word "walk" in the above sentence with about a hundred other words. It is painful to write this, but Ella will readily and truthfully tell you I gave Louis much more of my attention and time than I gave her.

I think any parent can understand why I did give my son more attention, but I have come to learn that, because of the extra time Louis received, Ella actually felt I loved him more. Of course, I did not love one child more than another, but I did treat them differently, and her needs were often seen as secondary. I also babied Louis more, whether it was because he allowed me to, he needed me to, or I just enjoyed doing it.

When Louis was ten, I was probably still treating him in some ways like he was much younger. For example, I would hold his hand in the grocery store if he wanted or kiss him on the cheek before he got on the bus. Ella would have never let me baby her beyond an appropriate age, but nevertheless she was jealous. What she saw was Louis getting more special attention and thus more love.

In addition to the extra time and affection, there was also the extra praise. Whenever Louis did something we weren't sure he could ever learn to do, my husband and I got overly excited. For example, the first time he took a step on his own, we called friends and family with the good news. My daughter was quick to point out that no one even noticed when she took her first step. Of course we did, but I got the message.

I wasn't the only one guilty of this, as other family members and friends showered Louis with more affection as well from the first greeting to the last kiss goodbye. Giving gifts was particularly problematic. People loved giving gifts to Louis. I think one reason was that my son got excited about almost any gift, and watching that brought joy to the giver. I can't count the number of times someone showed up at our house with just a gift for Louis. Granted, it was usually a very small present, but it was still a gift, and it was only for him. I finally had to instruct friends and family that, if they feel the need to give my son a gift, they must also offer my daughter one as well. I could no longer permit their joy and my son's delight to be more important than my daughter's hurt feelings.

Interestingly, many people just didn't understand this and thought I was being overly sensitive. People even suggested that Ella should be more grateful for her ability level and not to be so selfish to deny her sibling a simple joy. This is not the way I see it now after living with this dynamic for years. It is not okay to just acknowledge the child with disabilities in the family, even if the gift is small.

I think always being seen as second in needs and priority or feeling she is not noticed at all is one of the biggest shaping influences in my daughter's personality. She has felt in the shadows, loved less, and not seen as special. I wish I would have been more aware of her feelings and talked with her about them. She was grappling with complicated emotions, just like I was, but there was no one to talk to. And she didn't feel that she could come to me about her negative feelings toward her brother.

After she read a draft of this book, she wrote in the margins, "I felt bad about being angry at my brother because it wasn't his fault, but I still needed someone to blame. Most of the time, it was you, Mom."

She was also asked to straddle both worlds, just like I was. She had her realm with what she would call "normal" friends and families, and then she had the world with disabilities. Her friends had several questions about Louis she didn't always want to answer or explain. Some of her friends made fun of her brother and were repulsed by his behavior. Others showed him special attention and wanted to mother or dote on him like he was helpless.

While her friends complained about their annoying siblings, she felt she could never say anything bad about Louis to her friends. They expected her to be nice to him just because he had disabilities. She got the message loud and clear from all those around her: she needed to be kind to her brother who was less fortunate than she was.

Siblings have their own grief to process as well. I know she mourns over not having a brother with whom she can share typical experiences. I've learned my daughter has thought about having children of her own and feels loss over her brother not being the uncle she expected or her children not having first cousins to get to know. I know she worries deep down about who is going to take care of her brother when and if something happens to her parents. I know she loves her brother fiercely and still feels bad about the embarrassment, resentment, anger, jealousy, and guilt that boils up sometimes.

My daughter still struggles with her perceived unfairness of it all. She has a different set of rules than her brother does. I expect her to do chores that her brother is unable to do. I require her to help parent her older brother, to watch him when I am out, and to keep an eye out for him. She is more his second mother than his sister, and she feels that responsibility. She has grown up faster than was intended while her brother has lagged behind, which has made for complicated family dynamics.

In hindsight, I should have thought more about how I was parenting and carved out more time for my daughter without having her brother with us all the time. I should have made her needs come first more of the time and set aside more time to try to talk to her about her feelings. Many hospitals and agencies offer different types of groups for siblings of special needs children. I should have insisted my daughter become a part of one or found a counselor with whom she could process her emotions.

However, now that my daughter is sixteen, she is strong and resilient and has learned many important and beautiful lessons from being raised in a family with a child with a developmental disability. She has a wide-open acceptance of people who are different from her. She is more patient with and comfortable around people with disabilities. Louis has given her depth and character beyond her age as she learned early on that life is not perfect or fair. Living in this unabashedly imperfect family has taught her she doesn't have to be perfect. Her life will be shaped immeasurably by disabilities, just like mine and yours. It really is a remarkable, indelible imprint on a person's character.

The other important family relationship that changed unexpectedly was with my husband. If you have a partner, expect stress in that relationship. While it is unclear from the research as to whether or not couples with special needs children have a higher incidence of divorce, it is clear that parenting requires more of your attention and time. Decide as a couple how you will handle the inevitable stress and disagreement over parenting. Make a decision early on to protect and invest in your relationship.

In my own situation, before I found a community of other mothers raising children with disabilities, I didn't feel I could talk to anyone except my husband about how I was feeling. Fortunately that pattern didn't last long because we both realized our relationship deserved better. I knew I needed to talk to someone else about my feelings and encouraged my husband to do the same, as his loss in expectations and fear of the future was just as great as mine was. It may have been even more so because of the special father/son relationship he imagined.

So we started planning regular date nights. Every Friday, I would have a standing arrangement with a childcare provider for a few hours. Sometimes we just took a walk or grabbed a sandwich somewhere. Other times we would get dressed up and have a nice dinner and a movie. We agreed not to talk about disabilities and parenting. It was a night we both looked forward to. It was vital for keeping our identity as a couple.

Parenthood, especially when you have a child with a developmental disability, can take every ounce of your energy, which can surely leave you and your relationship with your partner depleted. Don't let disabilities become your only focus of attention for the rest of your life. Your relationship deserves more than that. Before you became parents, you were a couple who enjoyed doing things together. Try to continue to be a couple that is defined by more than being parents of a child with disabilities. Don't lose yourself or your partner in this parenting journey.

Helpful Suggestions

- Pay attention to the needs of other family members. Carve out time to spend with them without your child with disabilities.

- Consider how other members of the family feel about the child with special needs.

- Reflect on how the child with disabilities is treated compared to his or her siblings. Ask about perceived fairness, affection, and love.

- Encourage family members to attend support groups.

- Plan date nights with your partner and agree not to talk about disabilities.

Practice Self-Compassion

You will make thousands and thousands of decisions as a parent, and not every single one is going to be a good one. You will make mistakes. Even the very best parents fail and continue to make errors. Even parents with the easiest children fail and continue to make missteps. You may even make more. How on earth could you possibly have a clue about what is in store for you? You can't be perfect, and it will not be a pristine path. Things will get messy, and you will get lost. Learn to have self-compassion and self-forgiveness. No one expects you to know the right thing to do at every given time. Sometimes the best we can do is guess.

Looking back, I needed to grant more self-compassion and self-forgiveness in many places. For one, I didn't always like my child, and I felt like a horrible mother for having those feelings. I know I always felt a deep love for my child, but many times I just didn't like him. At times I was embarrassed by him. Occasionally I resented him for what I had decided to give up in order to raise him.

For example, Louis would bang his head against the wall in frustration over not being understood and demanded that only I comfort him. I admitted to a friend that I wasn't sure I liked my child and I needed a few days without him. After it came out of my mouth, I felt like crawling under a rock. I would imagine most mothers feel like this at some point in parenting, but maybe it was met—or I felt it was met—with more judgment because I was talking about a child with disabilities, a vulnerable child the world was supposed to have more compassion for.

And I was compassionless. I wanted typical things to dislike my child over, like talking back to me or slamming a door. Forgive yourself for this. You're not a bad mother if you don't like your child all the time or need a break.

Another area of self-compassion and forgiveness focused on my feelings that somehow my son's disability was my fault. I thought maybe I had carelessly allowed myself to be exposed to some toxin. Or maybe it was the two glasses of wine I drank before I knew I was pregnant. I ate raw tuna once when I was pregnant. Could that have caused it? How could I have been so negligent? I thought, if I had been better, smarter, and stronger, I would have had a child without brain damage.

Tell yourself that you're not to blame for your child's disability. Don't blame yourself, and if you do, learn to forgive yourself.

Finally, at times I was resentful of other people's seemingly perfect families, and I knew I shouldn't have been. Of course they weren't perfect, and I was certainly being overly sensitive. If you are feeling resentful, ask yourself what needs to change in your own situation for you to be happy for others. Be curious about why you feel a certain way. Put judgment of both others and yourself aside; let the feelings pass. There will always be families seemingly better off or worse off than yours. Remember—people may be looking at your family and possibly feeling resentful because you don't appear to have as many challenges as they do.

As you learn to accept your child with all his or her limitations, don't forget about accepting yourself for all of yours. You are worthy of love, belonging, and forgiveness just as much as anyone else. Studies show that you will be less anxious and depressed if you show yourself kindness and understanding as opposed to being self-critical.

When you do feel self-judgmental and self-critical, try to slow down your thought process, take a few deep breaths, and engage in a behavior you find relaxing. Common self-care rituals that help me be more self-compassionate are a hot bath, a good book, a long walk, and journal writing. Ask yourself what your self-care rituals are and how you can make them a routine part of your life.

Remember you are doing the best you can. You are making the best decisions you can based on the information available to you at the time. You can't change the past, you can't predict the future, and you just have this present moment in which to work. Don't get caught up in what you think other parents think of you. Other mothers and fathers do not have the same information you do; they also have different children and dissimilar circumstances. What is right or works for one parent/family/child may not be appropriate for you. Trust your gut, work with the information you have, act on it, and then forgive yourself if things don't work out. We all make lots of mistakes.

Helpful Suggestions

- Learn to forgive yourself for your mistakes.
- Don't blame yourself for your child's disability.
- Be curious about why you may feel resentment, jealousy, or envy.
- Engage in acts of self-care that feel right for you.
- Choose to be kind and have patience with yourself.

Forgive Other People

For the most part, I believe people mean well. I try to give all persons the benefit of the doubt and assume they do not mean to be insensitive. However, people say and do insensitive things when it comes to persons with disabilities. Mostly without realizing it and often stemming from good intention or possibly ignorance, remarks people make can sometimes come across the wrong way. There is even a Facebook page just for "stupid things people say to people with disabilities."

You will probably be offended at times on this parenting journey. Oftentimes people have absolutely no idea they have said something that could be offensive, while others apologize profusely because they realize as soon as it came out of their mouth that it was inappropriate. Sometimes people haven't said anything insensitive at all, yet they apologize just in case it came out wrong.

I once had a mother apologize repeatedly over asking me the age of my child. When I answered her honestly, she realized he didn't function at an age-appropriate level, and she regretted or was uncomfortable that she brought it up. In reality, I was happy she actually acknowledged my child and asked me a question.

It took me a long time to understand that some people are genuinely uncomfortable being around and talking about disabilities, so they try to avoid both you and your child. Many times people would actually ignore my child completely, desperately trying hard to keep the conversation away from children and parenting. The interactions where nothing was said left me feeling that my child was the elephant in the room everyone was tiptoeing around.

The comments that bothered me the most were the ones that I felt stemmed from pity. I sensed it in subtle gestures like "It will be okay" as they were leaving, even though there was never any mention of what needed to "be okay." Many of the insensitive comments I interpreted as coming from the "I'm glad it's you and not me" mentality. I wanted to respond to those remarks with an acknowledgement that my life is not bad, families regroup, life goes on, and it comes with many unforeseen blessings and graces. Instead I would just smile. My advice is to develop thick skin and remember that most people are kind and don't intend to offend you. Forgive and let it go. You have much better uses for your time and energy.

Helpful Suggestions

- Assume people don't intend to be insensitive with their remarks.

- Understand that many people are uncomfortable bringing up and discussing disabilities.

- Choose not to let other people's remarks or silence disturb your peace.

- Forgive and let it go. Use your time and energy in better places.

Live in the Present, but Prepare for the Future

You have probably heard this before, "Be more mindful. There is only this moment, and it is now. Live in the present." This mind-set is especially relevant for parents of children with developmental disabilities because, if you don't already, you will probably have some fear of the future. Try not to let your fear of the future interfere with enjoying the present.

I always go back to one example when I need to be reminded to live in the present and not to fear the future. When Louis was about thirteen months old, he hadn't managed to start feeding himself yet, and swallowing food was a huge issue for him. We were working with a feeding specialist, and he was making slow progress, but I would spend hours a day trying to get him to eat.

One day I just broke down, called my husband at work, and sobbed on the phone that our son was never going to be able to feed himself, he was going to need a feeding tube, and I was going to spend the rest of my life feeding him. I had worked myself into a frenzy of anxiety that proved no good to anyone or anything. I remember it being one of my lowest moments and ruining more than just my day. Today, he can practically eat an entire lasagna all by himself at one sitting. Feeding himself was a painstakingly slow skill for him to develop, but he got there.

I know people who seem emotionally unable to move on from the past or to stop stressing about the future. They struggle their whole life to be more present-focused. Probably because of my son's brain damage, he has a remarkably deep inner peace and has the ability to simply "be." Because he lives in the now every day, he has been my constant teacher on how to exist in the moment. I am greeted every morning with a "this is where I am right now" message that I have learned to appreciate. Some would say I am truly blessed.

When I remind myself that the future only exists in my imagination, it helps ease my anxiety. The future may be good, or it may not, but you have better uses for your time and energy than worrying about it.

Having said that, you also need to prepare for the future. As with all child-rearing, it goes quickly. You should think about a plan for the future, even though you know it may constantly be changing as you get new information and go through different transitions. Start an ongoing discussion early on about your ideas and dreams for your child with your community of support, health care professionals who you trust, and educators who have your best interests at heart. Start gathering information early about resources that may exist for your child down the road.

In my own case, a good case manager was critical to effectively plan for the future. As discussed earlier, it is important to get a child with developmental disabilities registered with state and local agencies, at which time you will probably be assigned a case manager. At least a yearly update with this person is important for documenting your child's progress, goals, and plans for the future. A case manager should help you understand what services are needed as well as where, when, and how they're provided. In addition, this person should help guide you to resources and programs that are in line with the goals and future plans you have for your child.

There are many professional agencies skilled at advising parents on financial issues related to preparing the future for special needs children. My husband and I met with a lawyer and estate planner in the early years of Louis's life to start figuring out a strategy to financially save for him. We asked other parents we knew who were in similar situations who they liked and then called around to compare costs and services.

Every five years, we revisit our plans and change them accordingly. We have also discussed with family and friends options for Louis's care if and when we are no longer available to care for him ourselves. We don't have a perfect plan in place because we really don't know what the future holds, but we feel as prepared as possible based on the information we have available right now.

Our long-term goal for Louis is to have him live in a community with others who have developmental disabilities and for him to have meaningful work. While I once thought Louis may be able to live independently with some support, as he aged, it became clear his skills would not progress to the level where we felt comfortable letting him live independently. Also his personality became more clear to us as he grew up, and we realized he's happiest when he is with others with developmental disabilities. We have no idea what any of this will look like, and it is easy to get caught up in the anxiety about not having a clear plan, but I have to trust that it will work out.

What I have been doing for the last few years is checking with agencies in my area about programs they offer for adults with disabilities. I ask every parent I meet who has an adult child with disabilities what he or she is doing or planning on doing. I am clear with his teachers, doctors, and therapists what our hopes are for his future. We have started to tour programs and facilities that may be a possibility. None of these tours are easy, as it is painful for me think about him not living with us, but I know it is an important step in preparing for the future.

Helpful Suggestions

- Don't let fear of the future interfere with enjoying the present.
- Develop a good relationship with your child's case manager.
- Start gathering information early about programs and resources that may be appropriate for your child in the future.
- Trust that time, experience, and knowledge will help you grow more confident about the future.

Don't Miss the Joy

The last thing I want to tell you is the most important: Don't miss the joy! It may be wrapped in something so different than what you expected, but it is there. Find it, cherish it, and surrender to it. There came a time when I stopped fighting my child's disability and I came to accept it. It was a hard-won balancing act, and it might have taken longer than I would have liked to get there, but I promise you that it's a wonderful place. I now accept who my child is and all his imperfections, and I understand who I am mothering him and all my imperfections. I focus on what my child can do and celebrate those abilities, no matter how small. That doesn't mean I stop trying to push myself and my child forward, but I am less concerned about the outcome, and I am more focused on the process.

I am also mindful of trying to create more opportunities for joy based on who my son is as an individual. For example, when he turned sixteen, he asked if he were going to get to drive because he knew that was the typical age to get a driver's license. Because he gets so excited about trying new things, we agreed he could drive one time. We found a big, open field with a gravel road running through it. Somehow my husband sat in the driver's seat with him, and Louis got to drive the car. He was laughing so hard and beaming from ear to ear. His joy filled his whole body and everyone else's who was watching. That memory will always make me smile, and I call upon it when I need a lift in spirits.

Raising a child with a disability has also taught me to value things differently. For example, one wonderful quality Louis has is that he doesn't hold back his excitement and love for life and other people. When someone shows up at the house for a visit, he greets everyone like a long-lost friend, with more joy and enthusiasm than he or she would probably receive from any other person. He is not afraid or inhibited to show people how much he loves them or to show his excitement for their successes. When we go bowling, he gets just as much thrill when someone else gets a strike as he would if he got one. His excitement, laughter, and joy over life can fill a room and your heart quite easily. The same goes when he receives a gift. As we know, a present really isn't about the money one spends but the thought that went into it. Louis doesn't care about what things costs, and he has very little understanding of money. He would be just as excited over a one-dollar gift as he would with a hundred-dollar one. I don't have to spend a certain amount on any of his gifts for him to feel he is loved or valued or for me to feel that I am a worthy giver. Feeling connected to people and showing them unabashed love are more important to him than anything else is. It is good for me to be frequently reminded of that.

I've learned so much about love on this journey. There is no way of predicting what is in store for you, but I do predict that you will learn to love in ways you never thought imaginable. You will learn to love the imperfect. One of the many gifts that come with a child with disabilities is the inevitable freedom from the pursuit of perfection. For me, this is one of the biggest gifts. You will also be loved in ways you never imagined. The love your child with developmental disabilities shows you and others may be truly unconditional. You will be loved for who you are, not what you look like, where you live, or what you can buy.

Louis sees all people as equal, without comparison, and regardless of circumstance. I think he also perceives himself as whole and beautiful just the way he is. You will be loved for being you, with all your imperfections. This is such a beautiful gift—pure, simple, transparent, and rare. Unfortunately too many people never get the chance to feel that type of love.

I never expected or wanted to be a mom raising a child with developmental disabilities. I would have given everything I had if someone could have taken away the brain damage of my child. As I stated many times in this book, I was frightened about the unknown and whether or not I could handle it. Ironically, if I had the choice now after almost twenty years to take away my son's brain damage and be left with a typically developing child, I wouldn't do it. I would miss him too much. I would miss how he makes me laugh, how he makes me feel, and how he loves me like no one else. More than anything though, I would worry I wouldn't have become who I am now because of him. I have become a better person because of raising a child with a disability. I often remind myself of a metaphor of a lotus flower growing in a murky pond. Out of this murkiness I found myself in, something beautiful has bloomed, and not only am I a witness to it, I am forever changed at my core for noticing it and being a part of it. I guarantee you will be transformed for the better while raising your child, if you let yourself be.

Let your child be your teacher and reap the joys and benefits that will come. Know that you are going on a different path than you had planned, but a valuable one, a route that is filled with much beauty and joy. Enjoy the journey when you can, and for the times you cannot, know that you are not alone.

Helpful Suggestions

- Give up the pursuit of perfection.
- Look for the joy in each day.
- Create opportunities for joy.
- Appreciate what you're learning and how you're changing from raising your child.
- Remind yourself often of the beautiful qualities in your child.
- Count your gifts and give thanks.
- Know you are not alone.

Practical Tips

I compiled this list from many parents' answers to what was most helpful when it came to the actual process of raising a child with a developmental disability.

A Medical Journal

Keep a medical/development journal. You think you will remember what a doctor or therapist said, what medicine was prescribed, what the name of the specialist was, or what age your child did this or that. However, all of this can become blurry over time. Over the years, you will be asked many questions about developmental milestones,

105

medicines, and appointments with specialists. You will thank yourself at one point for your note taking. Also if something would ever happen to you, a lot of information you would otherwise have stored in your head is now in a notebook for someone else to see.

Doctors' Appointments

The roughly fifteen minutes you get to see doctors need to be well spent, so be prepared. Try to have a list of questions written down for your doctor appointments and take notes. Oftentimes there is so much information coming at you that, while still needing to be mindful of your child's needs, your mind can't process it all. It helps to have someone else with you to take notes and interpret what the doctor said. If you are alone, record the doctor's visits on your phone. That way, when you are ready, you can play the recording to see what you missed. This also allows other people to hear what the doctor said and help you process the information.

Dressing Your Child

Find clothes that maximize independence and, at the same time, help your child to fit in socially. The reality is that people judge your child on appearance. Control what you can, and figure out what clothes work best based on ability level and age appropriateness, but still let him or her have his or her personal style when he or she can.

Planning for Transitions

Two big common transition periods are when your child turns three and five. Typically, at age three, your child will transition to public school services. Think about which school district best fits the needs of your child with disabilities and that of your other children. You may want to think about this early if it involves moving into that district. Call around, schedule tours, and talk to other parents about their school choices.

At age five, kindergarten and services during the school day typically begin. Think about which services your child needs to thrive. Find someone in the school system you trust and who will help you advocate for the needs of your child. Ask that person to be part of the Individual Evaluation Plan (IEP) process to ensure your child gets his or her needs met. In IEP meetings, the types of therapy and the time allotted to each therapy is determined.

While each school district is different, all public schools are required to provide a free and appropriate education to students with disabilities based on their individualized educational needs. The services may include special education and related aids and services such as physical, occupational, and speech therapy. Modifications to the regular education program also include adjustments in test-taking procedures and adjustments to rules regarding absences when a student's nonattendance is due to a disability. All of this information can be accessed at the federal government disability website at www.disability.gov.

Starting School

When your child starts school, a whole new stress level can pop up. It's one thing to deal with your own expectations and frustrations, but now you are sending your child out in the world for six hours a day. It is a world with potentially mean kids and lots of people you have no control over. One strategy for helping with this transition is, during the first week of school, to come into your child's classroom and answer any questions students might have about the disability. Most often the questions are based in kindness and caring. Having inquiries answered can take away the mystery surrounding a disability and can set the tone for it being okay to talk about disability in general. You may find that the classmates go home and educate their parents about disabilities. Depending on your child, you may find it better to have him or her as part of the conversation or not in the classroom during the discussion. In addition, you may choose to send a letter home to the parents of the class, introducing your child to them and encouraging them to ask any questions of you that they or their child may have.

Another helpful strategy is a letter about your child to be given to all the teachers in the school. It could highlight your child's strengths and weaknesses, your family, and what he or she likes to do. In just one piece of paper, you can relay through photos and text that your child is a multidimensional person. Teachers will thank you for helping them understand your child better. It also shows that you are a parent very invested in your child fitting in at school and one who is paying attention to what is going on. This strategy may also be helpful for any activities the child participates in such as after-school programs or sports where volunteer coaches may not be trained in working with kids with disabilities.

Websites

Many websites have been created for parents of children with special needs. Listed below are a few well-recognized ones, all of which have links to valuable resources.

Exceptional Parent, www.eparent.com

The mission of Exceptional Parent (eparent) is to develop, translate, and share information for positive change for the special needs community. It has both a monthly print magazine and a website. It is an excellent resource for the most up-to-date information for families of children and adults with disabilities.

Parent to Parent USA, www.p2pusa.org

Parent to Parent USA is a national nonprofit organization committed to providing emotional and informational support to families of children who have special needs by matching parents seeking support with an experienced, trained Support Parent.

Circle of Moms, www.circleofmoms.com

Circle of Moms is an online community for moms seeking connection to other mothers in a similar situation. One can choose from countless community groups in which to participate.

Parenting Special Needs Magazine, www.parentingspecialneeds.org

This is an online magazine providing parents of children with special needs of all ages and stages of life with both information and inspiration.

Family Voices, www.familyvoices.org

Family Voices is a national, nonprofit, grassroots organization promoting quality health care for children with special needs. It's an excellent resource for local, state, and federal programs and policy.

eSpecial Needs, www.especialneeds.com

eSpecial Needs is an online company whose mission is to make life easier for parents and children by providing innovative, hard-to-find, high-quality products for children with special needs. They are an excellent resource for new products and have links to funding organizations and resources by state.

About the Author

Mary Kay DeGenova, Ph.D., is the mother of a child with developmental disabilities. She received her Ph.D. from Purdue University and is a former associate professor of Child Development and Family Studies. Her other books include *Intimate Relationships, Marriages, and Families* and *Families in Cultural Context.* She lives in St. Louis with her husband and two children.

CPSIA information can be obtained
at www.ICGtesting.com
Printed in the USA
LVOW13s2300080418
572753LV00006B/106/P